# Really Useful English Grammar

## Jake Allsop

Penguin Quick Guides Series Editors:
Andy Hopkins and Jocelyn Potter

D1343126

Pearson Education Limited
Edinburgh Gate
Harlow
Essex CM20 2JE, England
and Associated Companies throughout the world.

ISBN 978-0-582-46893-1

First published 2001
Fourth impression 2008
Copyright © Jake Allsop 2001

The moral right of the author has been asserted.

Produced for the publisher by Bluestone Press, Charlbury, UK.
Designed and typeset by White Horse Graphics, Charlbury, UK.
Illustrations by Roger Fereday (Linda Rogers Associates).
Photography on pages 11, 53, 103 and 129 by Patrick Ellis. All others by
Bluestone Press
Printed and bound in China
EPC/04

Published by Pearson Education Limited in association with Penguin Books
Ltd, both companies being subsidiaries of Pearson plc.

For a complete list of the titles available from Penguin English visit
our website at www.penguinenglish.com, or please write to your local
Pearson Education office or to: Penguin English Marketing Department,
Pearson Education, Edinburgh Gate, Harlow, Essex CM20 2JE.

# Contents

Making comparisons  *bigger/biggest; more/the most expensive*
Patterns with adjectives  *I'm falling asleep.*
Defining clauses  *She's a woman who knows everything.*
Adjective order  *a big old Victorian house*

Key facts about verbs
Actions and states • Time • Viewpoint
Simple and continuous tenses  *The bus leaves at eight.*
*They've been working hard.*
Forming questions  *Must you leave? Why didn't you call?*
Forming negatives  *She didn't play last week.*
Short forms  *You're Harry, aren't you?*
Irregular verbs  *speak/spoke/spoken; find/found/found;*
*put/put/put*

Key facts about tenses
Simple present • Simple past • Continuous tenses
Perfect tenses • Ways of expressing the future

# Grammar files

# Answers

# Getting started

Most grammar books are thick and heavy – and too big to carry around in your pocket or your bag! *Really Useful English Grammar* contains the key facts that you need to know to be able to use English correctly. You can take it anywhere with you, leaving the bigger grammar book at home for later reference.

## What's in this book?

- Chapters 1 to 8 cover the main areas of the language. Each chapter begins with **Key Facts**, illustrated with examples from contemporary spoken English. There are exercises and a **Review** to test your understanding.

- Chapter 9, *Frequently asked questions*, deals with some of the common confusions that occur: for example, the use of *make* and *do*, the difference between *should* and *ought to*. There is also a series of sentences containing common errors for you to identify and correct.

- The chapters are followed by three **Grammar files** that provide straightforward information on verb forms, including a list of irregular verbs, and useful prepositional phrases.

- At the back of the book, there is an **Answers** section for all the exercises and review activities.

## How can I use the book?

- As a quick reference for those occasions when you are not completely sure about a point of grammar.

- To refresh and test your knowledge when you have a little time to spare.

- You can work through the book systematically, from cover to cover, or just dip into it, concentrating on those points that matter to you at the time.

In trying to fix a grammatical rule in your head, it is always a good idea to memorise an example sentence. So, for example, don't simply learn '*going to* expresses intention'; learn a sentence like *I'm going to ask my boss for a raise*. You can learn the sentences in this book, then try making up your own, so that they are *real* for you. But remember, while *Really Useful English Grammar* contains essential information about English grammar, it does not tell the whole story. For detailed grammar advice you should also consult a good reference grammar.

# Nouns
# and
# pronouns

1

# Key facts about nouns

Nouns describe concrete things that you can see or touch: *a friend, a house, a church*; and abstract things that you cannot see or touch: *happiness, information, love, time*.

## 1 Plurals

- To form the plural of most nouns add -*(e)s*: *friend–friends, house–houses, church–churches*
- Nouns ending in -*ch*, -*sh*, -*s*, -*ss* , -*x* add -*es*: *match–matches, wish–wishes, bus–buses, kiss–kisses, box–boxes*
- Nouns ending in consonant + *y* change the *y* to *i* and add -*es*: *baby–babies, country–countries* (Vowel + *y* just add -*s*: *boy–boys*)
- Most nouns ending in -*f* change the *f* to *v* and add -*es*: *wife–wives, shelf–shelves*

13

- Note these irregular plurals:
  *man–men, woman–women, child–children, foot–feet, mouse–mice, tooth–teeth*

- The nouns *police* and *people* are plural in English.
  *The police have arrived; people are angry.*

- Food, substances and materials are always singular.
  *bread, milk, grass, snow, steel, cotton, glass*

- Abstract nouns are also always singular.
  *love, happiness, information*

 Note that these words are singular in English:
*news, advice, furniture, work, homework, progress, luggage*
*Hard work is good for you.*
*No news is good news.*

## 2 Possession

- To show possession by people or animals, add -*'s* or -*(s)'*: *the boy's bicycle, women's rights, girls' magazines*

   Use this form with time expressions: *in three days' time, yesterday's newspaper*

- In other cases, use compound nouns (see below): *bedroom, computer program, washing machine*
  or the preposition *of*: *a cup of tea, the leg of a table*

## 3 Compound nouns

- The first part describes the second part: *toothbrush* = a *brush* used for cleaning *teeth*

- Write compound nouns as one word where both parts are very short: *homework, bedroom, toothbrush*

# Practice 1A

## A Complete the table.

| | Singular | Plural |
|---|---|---|
| 1 | | women |
| 2 | life | |
| 3 | | feet |
| 4 | child | |
| 5 | day | |
| 6 | | ladies |
| 7 | match | |
| 8 | book | |
| 9 | | taxes |
| 10 | tree | |

**B Choose the correct form of the verb.**

1 People *is/are* always ready to criticise.
2 Antique furniture *cost/costs* a lot.
3 The news from the war zone *is/are* not good.
4 Your hair *look/looks* really nice!
5 The police *has/have* asked for volunteers.

**C Combine words from boxes 1 and 2 to make compound nouns.**

| 1 | 2 |
|---|---|
| 1 arm | car |
| 2 bottle | chair |
| 3 green | directory |
| 4 match | driver |
| 5 police | house |
| 6 post | office |
| 7 screw | opener |
| 8 telephone | stick |
| 9 wrist | watch |

# Key facts about pronouns

## 1 He/she/it/they

These pronouns replace people or things that have already been referred to.

*Jane's a police officer.* **She** *loves her job.*

| Subject | Object | Possessive | |
|---------|--------|------------|------|
| he | him | his | his |
| she | her | her | hers |
| it | it | its | – |
| they | them | their | theirs |

*Mary is an engineer;* **she** *works in a factory; it suits* **her***; she likes* **her** *job.*

**They** *live in an old house; it suits* **them***; they love* **their** *house; they love* **it***.*

*Jane's a
police officer.
She loves
her job.*

## 2 I/we/you

*I* (written with a capital I) refers to the person speaking; *we* refers to more than one person speaking; *you* refers to the person or people spoken to.

| Subject | Object | Possessive | |
|---------|--------|------------|------|
| Who? | Who(m)? | Whose? | |
| I | me | my | mine |
| we | us | our | ours |
| you | you | your | yours |

*I'm hungry; make **me** a sandwich for **my** lunch.*
*We have a dog; it lives with us; it is **our** pet.*
*You must take money with **you** on **your** journey.*

* Use *you* for one person or for several people:
  *John, **you** are a real friend.*
  *Boys and girls, I want **you** to listen to me.*

* Parts of *be, have,* etc., can join with pronouns: *I'm, you're, he's, they're, I've, she'd, we'll*
* Distinguish between *its* – *a house and its garden*; and *it's* – *it's [it is] a nice house*)

*Boys and girls, I want you to listen to me.*

## 3 -self/-selves

> myself, yourself, himself, herself, itself
> ourselves, yourselves, themselves

- Use *-self/-selves* when subject and object are the same.
  *They like to enjoy **themselves** at weekends.*
  *Make **yourself** at home!*

- The *-self/-selves* form is also used for emphasis.
  *Nobody helped me. I did it **myself**!*
  *The house **itself** is small, but the garden is big.*

 Note: *by myself* = alone, without help

*The house itself is small, but the garden is big.*

## 4 Special uses of the pronoun *it*

- The pronoun *it* is used in many patterns:
  *It's raining, it's a nice day, it's 2 o'clock.*
  *It's easy/hard/difficult to know what to do.*

  Note the pattern with *there*:
  *There's a lot to do; there's a spider in my bed.*

- Use object pronouns as direct and indirect objects:
  DIRECT    *He loves **me**.*
  INDIRECT  *Tell **me** a story.*

  After *explain* and *say*, use *to me*:
  *Explain this to me; say hello to your grandma.*

## 5 Possessives

Use *my*, etc., with a following noun:
***Your** hair looks nice; I don't like **my** hair.*

Use *mine*, etc., when no noun follows:
***Yours** is much nicer than **mine**.*

# Practice 1B

## A Complete the table.

| I | me | | | |
|------|------|-------|--------|------------|
| you | | | yours | |
| he | | his | | |
| she | her | | | |
| it | | | | itself |
| we | us | | | ourselves |
| they | | their | | |

## B Choose the correct word.

1 This bike belongs to me. It is *my/mine* bike.
2 Mary's my sister, so I'm *his/her* brother.
3 We really enjoyed *us/ourselves* at the disco.
4 Have the girls finished *her/their* homework?
5 Did you get a letter from Alan and *I/me* today?
6 Is this John's work, or is it *your/yours*?

# Review 1

**Correct the mistakes in these sentences.**

1 ✗ Did she go to the party by her own?

_____

2 ✗ Its time to give the cat it's dinner.

_____

3 ✗ Look after yourself, children!

_____

4 ✗ Explain me the difference between _if_ and _when_.

_____

5 ✗ Is this your hairs' brush?

_____

6 ✗ It's not much bread left.

_____

7 ✗ Did Kate say you where she was going?

_____

8 ✗ Your house is bigger than our.

_____

# Determiners

# Key facts about determiners

Determiners often identify, and describe distribution and quantity. They come before nouns.

## 1 Identifying

| a/an, the, this/these, that/those |
| --- |

They answer the question *Which one(s)?*
*I'm looking for **a** book.*
*I'm looking for **the** book that my dad bought me.*
*Is **this** the book you want?* (i.e. this one here)
*No, I want **that** book.* (i.e. the one further away)

### a(n)/the

- *a(n)* is not used in plural statements:
  *A dog is a good pet* or *Dogs are good pets.*
- Use *some* as the plural of *a(n)* for an unspecified number or quantity:
  *I bought an overcoat and **some** shirts.*

- Use *the* for something that is well-known:
  *I must go to **the** bank and **the** post office.*
  ***The** poor just get poorer.* (= poor people)

- Don't use *the* in general statements:
  *Sugar is bad for you. Dogs make good pets.*
  … or in many verb/preposition + noun expressions:
  *have lunch, make friends, for example, by train*

*Dogs make good pets.*

## 2 Describing distribution

| all   each   every   both   either/neither |

These words are used to describe groups:
*Every* morning, I give *each* of my children a kiss
and they *all* say 'Don't do that, daddy!'
*Both* knives are sharp; *either* will do.

- For three or more in a group, use *all/every*.
  For two or more in a group, use *each*.
  For two only in a group, use *both/either/neither*.

- Use *both/all* to join, *either/neither* to separate:
  *Both* roads lead to town; take *either* of them.

- Use *every* and *each* to describe the group as
  individuals (*every* = a series, *each* = one by one).
  *Every* Saturday, we go to the market.
  Take *each* day as it comes.

*Every morning I give each of my children a kiss.*

31

Note the patterns with *all*:
pronoun + *all* or *all of* + pronoun
*he ate all the biscuits – he ate them all*
*all* + *the/my*, etc. + noun
*all my life, all these rules, all the students*

## 3 Describing quantity

> (not) much, (not) many, some, any, no, a few,
> a little, a lot of

They answer the questions *How much/many?*

*How **much** money have you got?*
*– I haven't got **much** money.*
*– I've got **a little**.*

*How **many** dollars have you got?*
*– I haven't got **any** dollars.*
*– I've got a **few** pesetas.*

*Are all these children yours?*

### some/any/no

- Use *some* in positive statements and in questions expecting the answer *yes*:
  *There's **some** milk in the fridge if you're thirsty.*
  *Would you like **some** biscuits with your milk?*

- Use *any* in negative statements and in open questions:
  *There isn't **any** milk in the fridge.*
  *Do you have **any** mineral water instead?*

- Use *no* if you want to emphasise the negative:
  *You're wrong: there's **no** milk in the fridge!*

- Use *some-/any-/no-* (and also *every-*) with *-thing/-one/-body/-where*.
  *Shh! Don't say **anything** to **anyone**!*
  *Let's go **somewhere** different for our holidays this year.*

# Practice 2

**A Put in *a/an* or *the* where needed.**

1 .... French people shake .... hands more often
   than .... English do.

2 .... Moon goes round .... Earth.

3 Let me give you .... piece of .... advice: don't
   accept .... sweets from .... strange men!

4 When I was .... boy, we always had .... eggs for ....
   breakfast.

5 What time do you leave .... home in .... morning?

6 *If* is .... poem by .... English writer.

**B Add *some*, *any* or *no* to these sentences.**

1 There's .... point in telling me; I can't do .... thing
   about it.

2 .... body's been smoking! I can smell it!

3 I have coffee but .... milk, so you'll have to drink
   it black.

4 Shall I make .... more popcorn for you?

5 I know hardly .... body at this party.

# Review 2

## A Correct the mistakes.

1 ✗ Are these money yours?
2 ✗ There aren't no cakes left. The cat has eaten all them.
3 ✗ We do any shopping every weekends.
4 ✗ I have three sons and they are both crazy.
5 ✗ Have you lived here your all life?
6 ✗ Why do French always shake the hands when they meet?

## B Replace the underlined word with the word in brackets, and change the sentences as necessary.

1 I need a few more <u>minutes</u> [time].
2 You should eat fewer <u>potatoes</u> [bread].
3 There aren't many <u>chairs</u> in here [furniture].
4 I haven't much <u>homework</u> to do [exercises].

# Adjectivals

# Key facts about adjectivals

Adjectivals tell you more about a noun. They define. They answer the question *Which one(s)?*

*Which man? The **tall** one.*
*Which houses? The **new** ones **across the road**.*

## 1 Ways of defining

Single items (usually adjectives): *new, tall, afraid, well-known*
Phrases: *the house **across the road***
Defining clauses: *a woman **who lived in a shoe***

## 2 Position

Adjectivals come…
- immediately before a noun:
  *a **silly** mistake; the **best** computers;*
  ***two new red cotton** dresses*
- after verbs like *be, seem, look, feel*:
  *I am **cold**; it seems **stupid**; she looks **happy**.*

These adjectives can only come after a verb: *afraid,
ashamed, asleep, awake, glad, ill, well*
*I felt ill yesterday, but I'm well again now.*
*As I'm afraid of the dark, I stayed awake all night.*

*You look
cold.*

## 3 Numbers

- The numbers *one, two, three,* etc. (cardinal numbers) answer the question *How many? There are **thirty-one** days in October.*

- The numbers *first, second, third,* etc. (ordinal numbers) answer the question *In what order? Today is the **thirty-first** of October.*

## 4 Adjectives from names

- Adjectives from the names of countries end in *-ese, -n/-an/-ian, -ish, -ch* or *-i:*
  *Chinese, Indian, Spanish, Iraqi*

- Adjectives from names of people mostly end in *-n/-an/-ian:*
  *Victoria–Victorian, Christ–Christian*

# 5 Making comparisons

- Add *-er/-est* to most one-syllable adjectives, and to two-syllable adjectives ending in *-le*, *-ly*, *-ow* and *-er*.
  *big–bigger, simple–simpler, lovely–lovelier*
  *The Taj Mahal is **older** than the Eiffel Tower.*
  *Who is **the youngest** member of the team?*

- Otherwise (or if you are not sure), use *more/most*: *more difficult, most interesting*.
  *Health is **more important** than money.*
  *She's the **most intelligent** person I know.*

 These are irregular:
*good–better–best, bad–worse–worst,*
*little–less–least, much/many–more–most*

*Are you sure your oldest player is under eleven?*

# 6 Patterns with adjectives

- With the verb *make*:
  *He made me very angry.*

- In verb + adjective patterns like:
  *fall asleep, go mad, grow old*

- In the pattern *It is* + adjective + *to do*:
  *This puzzle is too difficult for me to solve.*

- ending in -*ed* and -*ing*:
  *What a boring programme!*
  *Oh, aren't you interested in football?*

45

## 7 Defining clauses

- Clauses which define the subject begin with the pronoun *that*:

  *He's a man **that knows everything**.*

  *I have a car **that makes a loud noise**.*

  When the clause defines the object of the verb, leave out the pronoun *that*:

  *Mary is the girl + I told you about **her** –*

  *Mary is the girl (that) I told you about.*

  *That is the car + I sold **it** to Charlie –*

  *That's the car I sold to Charlie.*

- *Who* (for people) and *which* (for things) are less commonly used:

  *He's a man **who** knows everything.*

  *That's the car **which** I sold to Charlie.*

- *Whose* is used to show possession:

  *Are you the man **whose** car was stolen?*

I have a
car that
makes a
loud noise.

# 8 Adjective order

- Determiners and numbers come first:
  **all these** big green apples
  **my first** important assignment

- Order of adjectives is usually:

| | | |
|---|---|---|
| 1 | quality | *beautiful, dirty, nice* |
| 2 | size | *big, little, small* |
| 3 | age/heat | *old, young, cold* |
| 4 | shape | *square, round* |
| 5 | colour | *blue, red, dark* |
| 6 | origin | *French, Victorian* |
| 7 | material | *metal, plastic, cotton* |

A **big old Victorian** house.
A **beautiful round red metal** ball.

# Practice 3

## A Put the following in the correct order.

1 school/my/all/old/photos
2 dining/French/several/old/tables
3 wildlife/Mike's/African/first/safari
4 pretty/Brazilian/young/a lot of/girls
5 tennis/cotton/white/a pair of/shorts

## B Make comparisons like the following:

Example: English–Japanese     [easy]
*English is easier than Japanese.*

| | |
|---|---|
| 1 Japanese–English | [difficult] |
| 2 Walking–jogging | [healthy] |
| 3 Thirst–hunger | [bad] |
| 4 Health–money | [important] |
| 5 Half a loaf–no loaf at all | [good] |

## C Match verbs and adjectives.

1 fall      a) green
2 go        b) asleep
3 grow    c) sure
4 make    d) old
5 stand    e) still
6 turn     f) mad

## D Join the two sentences as in the example.

Example: You bought me a book. This is the book .....

*This is the book (that) you bought me.*

1 You wrote to a girl. I am the girl .....
2 I can speak Chinese. I am the only one .....
3 She works in a bank. She's the one .....
4 I told you about a man. He's the man .....
5 A cat ate my breakfast. This is the cat .....

# Review 3

**Correct the following sentences. There may be more than one mistake in each sentence.**

1 ✗ Never wake up an asleep tiger.

_____

2 ✗ It's the most biggest stadium of the world!

_____

3 ✗ Are you the man who's cat ate my breakfast?

_____

4 ✗ I am interesting in football. I go to all the matches.

_____

5 ✗ Today is the twenty-two of June.

_____

6 ✗ Angela is the more intelligent person I know.

_____

# Prepositions

# Key facts about prepositions

Prepositions go with nouns, pronouns and reflexives to form 'noun phrases'. These noun phrases provide useful expressions of:

| | |
|---|---|
| **place** | *into the house, under a tree* |
| **time** | *at 2 o'clock, on Sunday, by Friday, during the day* |

They express other relationships, such as:

| | |
|---|---|
| **purpose** | *work for the money, do anything for a friend* |
| **method** | *go by bus, leave by the back door* |
| **manner** | *in a hurry, like a fish, with a smile* |
| **possession** | *a man with a beard, a friend of mine* |

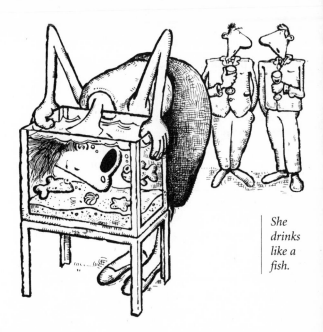

*She drinks like a fish.*

- After a preposition, use the -*ing* form of the verb:
  *good at **swimming**, tired of **waiting***

- After a preposition, use the object form of the pronoun:
  *for **them**, without **her**, near **us***

- Some verbs and adjectives are followed by a particular preposition:
  ***look for** an answer, **depend on** others, **talk about** the weather, **kind to** animals*

- Prepositions can come at the end of a question or a defining relative clause:
  *Is this the book you were referring **to**?*
  *What are you talking **about**?*

*I'm not very good at skiing!*

# 1 Place

> above, across, against, along, among, at, away from, behind, below, between, by, down, from, in, in front of, inside, into, near, next to, off, on, opposite, out of, over, past, round, through, to, towards, under, up

Prepositions of place answer the questions
*Where?* and *Where to/from?*
*I live in an apartment block **near** the city centre.*
*We walked **from** Land's End **to** John o'Groats.*

### in/at

Use *in* to emphasise a position inside a building
or other big space.
*It was raining, so we stayed **in the hotel** all day.*
*We met **at the Court Hotel**.*

*At the cinema there's always a tall person in front of you.*

### in/into/inside

- Use *into* to make clear the idea of moving and entering:
  We walked **into the room**; there was nobody **in the room**.

- *Inside* is more precise than *in* and always refers to an enclosed space:
  Stay **inside the car**, there are dangerous animals **outside**.

### over/under; above/below

- *Over* and *under* describe vertical position:
  A plane flew **over** the house; we sat **under** a tree.

- *Above* and *below* simply say that one thing is higher than another:
  **above** average height, **below** sea level

*He's above average height.*

## 2 Time

> after, at, before, by, during, for, from, in, on,
> past, since, to, until (till)

Time prepositions answer the questions *When?*
and *How long?*

### to/at/past

Use *to, at* and *past* to tell the time:
quarter **to** three, half **past** seven, **at** six o'clock
Also **at** night, **at** the weekend

### on

Use *on* with days and parts of the day and with
dates:
**on** Friday(s), **on** Monday afternoon, **on** the fourth
of July

**in**

Use *in* with parts of the day:
*in* the morning, *in* the afternoon, *in* the evening
(but *at* night)

**by**

Use *by* when you want to say *not later than*:
*If you haven't finished **by** six o'clock, I'll shoot you!*

*If he's not here by 11.20, it's all off.*

### since/for

- Use *since* to describe the starting point of an action:
  *I've been waiting **since** two o'clock.*

- Use *for* to describe the length of time of the action:
  *I've been waiting **for** two hours.*

### until (till)/during

- *Until* (or *till*) means up to a point in the future:
  *What happened to you? We waited for you **until** ten o'clock.*

- *During* means after the start and before the finish of an event.
  *Passengers are requested to switch off mobile phones **during** the flight.*

# Practice 4A

## A Choose the correct prepositions.

John walked (1) across/in the road, (2) past/to the church and (3) at/round the corner. Then he went (4) along/up the steps and (5) down/over the bridge. He walked (6) through/over the garden and (7) under/across the grass until he reached the footpath. Then he went (8) through/along the footpath, jumped (9) under/over the gate and went (10) into/at the bank.

## B Complete the sentences

1  (It is 12 now! It was 7 when I had breakfast.)
   I last ate .... seven o'clock. I haven't eaten .... seven o'clock. I haven't eaten .... five hours.
2  I was born .... 1980. I was born .... Friday 7 July at 3 o'clock .... the morning!

These words are used to describe other relationships – of purpose, method, manner and possession.

> about, according to, against, at, by, except, for, from, in spite of, instead of, like, of, than, with, without

## 3 Purpose

**for**

- Use *for* to describe why something is done:
  *This knife is **for** peeling potatoes.*
  *I've bought some medicine **for** your cold.*

- Also, use *for* to describe support:
  *Did you vote **for** the Republican candidate?*

- The opposite of *for* is *against*:
  *I am **against** the idea of closing the street to traffic.*

*They say
scientists have
found a cure
for apathy, but
nobody seems
to care.*

## 4 Method

**by/with/without**

Use *by/with/without* to describe how something is done:

*I opened the window **by** breaking the glass.*
*Can you open a bottle **with** your teeth?*
*I can do it **without** any help from you!*

Also, use *by* to describe authorship:
*'The Street Lawyer' **by** John Grisham*

## 5 Manner

**like/as**

- Use *like* to compare:
  *He fights **like** a tiger when he is angry.*

- Use *as* with adjectives:
  *I'm **as** hungry **as** a horse.*

*I'm as hungry as a horse.*

# 6 Possession

## of

- Use *of* to describe possession:
  *the symphonies of Mozart, a man of property*

- Also, use *of* to describe materials and quantities:
  *made of wood, a glass of water*

Note also the following:

| | |
|---|---|
| **Subject matter** | *about/on* |
| | *a book about web page design, a lecture on Turkish ceramics* |
| **Origin** | *from/out of* |
| | *This lamp was made from (out of) a bottle.* |
| **Comparisons** | *than* |
| | *My father is stronger than yours.* |

*This car was made from recycled parts.*

# Practice 4B

**Add a preposition to complete these phrases.**

1  a present .... your birthday
2  a painting .... Rembrandt
3  a table made .... wood
4  an old man .... a grey beard
5  a car that goes .... the wind
6  a book .... dinosaurs
7  a building taller .... the Eiffel Tower
8  a peace march .... the war
9  I am very proud .... my daughter.
10 He is very good .... football.
11 Did you pay .... the meal?
12 Does this pen belong .... you?
13 Bill looks exactly .... his father!
14 I'm not used .... eating spicy food.
15 Do you believe .... ghosts?

He's not used to eating spicy food!

# Review 4

## A Correct the mistakes in these sentences.

1 ✗ Please be home *until* 10 pm at the latest!
2 ✗ I have been waiting *since* two hours.
3 ✗ John got tired of *wait*, so he went home.
4 ✗ Our friends were late, so we went without *they*.
5 ✗ What did you do *in* the weekend?
6 ✗ 12.50 is the same as ten *past* one.
7 ✗ We arrived *to* the hotel after midnight.

## B Match the phrases.

1 A hammer is used
2 He started his car
3 John eats
4 She made a model
5 I hate to depend
6 He can talk

a) on other people.
b) without moving his lips.
c) for driving in nails.
d) by turning the key.
e) out of yoghurt cartons.
f) like a horse.

# Verbs 1:
# Form

5

# Key facts about verbs

Verbs describe the time of an event and our viewpoint or attitude to the event.

## Actions and states

Verbs can describe:

- physical actions – *sleep, live, talk, work, drive*
  Some people **work** to live, some **live** to work!

- mental actions – *think, dream, worry, wonder*
  I **wonder** if there is life on other planets.

- states – *be, seem, appear*
  You **seem** very sad today. Are you all right?

## Time

Verbs describe time (past, present, future):
I **lived** in Rio for years; now I **live** in São Paolo.

## Viewpoint

Verbs show whether the action is finished or unfinished, whether its outcome is certain or uncertain, etc.

- *I've lost my home.*
  (present result of past action)

- *Now I'm living with friends.*
  (an unfinished action)

- *It might rain later.*
  (predicting an action)

- *I'm going to marry a millionaire.*
  (expressing intention)

- *He's stupid.* (permanent state)
  *He's being stupid.* (temporary state)

79

# 1 Simple and continuous tenses

(For more information see **Grammar file 3**)

- There are two simple tenses (present and past)
  - Present: *talk* (*talks* with *he/she/it*)
    *Fashions **come** and **go**.*
    *Mary **works** in Cardiff; she **teaches** maths.*
  - Past: *talked*
    *The movie **started** half an hour ago.*

- The other tenses and forms use the base form
  *talk*, the present participle, *talking*, or the past
  participle, *talked* with:
  - Parts of *be* and *have*:
    *It **is raining**. It **has rained** every day this
    week!*
    *John **has been working** hard.*
  - Modals, e.g. *will, must, can/could, may/might*:
    *He **must leave** soon; he **could come** back
    later.*

## 2 Forming questions

- Invert subject and verb:
  *It is raining –* **Is it** *raining?*
  *He must leave –* **Must he** *leave?*
  *Where* **have you** *been?*

- Use parts of *do* in the simple tenses:
  *Where* **do you** *live? Where* **does she** *work?*
  *What* **did you** *do last night? Why* **didn't you** *call?*

## 3 Forming negatives

- Add **not** (**n't**)
  *It is not (isn't) too late to go out.*
  *I can't believe it.*
  *I haven't done much work today.*

- Use parts of *do* in the simple tenses:
  *I* **eat** *vegetables –* **I don't eat** *meat.*
  *He* **plays** *soccer – He* **doesn't play** *rugby.*
  *We* **drank** *coffee – We* **didn't** *drink tea.*

## 4 Short forms

- Parts of *be*, *have* and modals (e.g. *can*, *must*)
  join with *not*:
  *is + not = isn't*
  *had + not = hadn't*
  *can + not = can't*

   Note: *will + not = won't*

- Use short forms in
  - speech and informal writing
  - short answers
  *Does Carrie live here? No, she **doesn't**.*
  - question tags
  Expecting *yes*: *You're Harry, **aren't you**?*
  Expecting *no*: *This isn't right, **is it**?*

## 5 Irregular verbs

(See **Grammar File 3** for list.)

- There are about 140 irregular verbs in English,
  e.g. *speak, spoke, spoken*:
  I **speak** French. We **spoke** German at home.
  I haven't **spoken** French for ages.

- The main patterns are:

  **ABC** where the three parts are different:
  e.g.   *speak, spoke, spoken*          (about 55)

  **ABB** where two parts are the same:
  e.g.   *find, found, found*          (about 55)

  **AAA** where all three parts are the same:
  e.g.   *put, put, put*          (about 25)

# Practice 5

## A Complete the table.

|     | speak | spoke   | spoken  |
| --- | ----- | ------- | ------- |
| 1   | find  |         |         |
| 2   |       | caught  |         |
| 3   |       |         | fallen  |
| 4   | put   |         |         |
| 5   |       | saw     |         |
| 6   |       |         | written |
| 7   | tell  |         |         |
| 8   |       | took    |         |
| 9   |       |         | met     |
| 10  | cost  |         |         |

## B Complete the questions.

1 I went to the movies last night.
*Where did you go last night?*

2 I live in an apartment. Where .... ?

3 I had steak for dinner. What .... ?

4 I can speak three languages. How many .... ?

5 I go to work by car. How .... ?

6 I use Word 6. Which program .... ?

7 I have done nothing today! What .... ?

## C How many correct forms can you make from these tables?

1

| | | |
|---|---|---|
| It | has | move |
| | has been | moving |
| | will | moved |

2

| | | |
|---|---|---|
| Does | | work? |
| Did | she | works? |
| Has | | working? |
| Is | | worked? |

# Review 5

**Correct the following sentences. There may be more than one mistake in each sentence.**

1 ✗ What John does? He teachs physics.
_____

2 ✗ I'm tired: I've been work hard.
_____

3 ✗ Must we to stay in?
_____

4 ✗ Why this watch doesn't works?
_____

5 ✗ You're a student, isn't it?
_____

6 ✗ Can you telling me the time, please?
_____

7 ✗ This box is measuring 200cm by 300cm.
_____

8 ✗ Do you live here? Yes, I live.
_____

# Verbs 2: Tenses

6

# Key facts about tenses

This chapter covers the main uses of the simple present, simple past, continuous and perfect verb forms and ways of expressing the future.

## 1 Simple present

Time: not important, any time
Viewpoint: simply describes the action or the state
*Fish **swim**, birds **fly**. I **work** in an office.*

- Use the present simple:
  - to make general true statements
    *The earth **goes** round the sun.*
  - with verbs that describe mental states, possession, measurement, appearance:
    *Do you **understand**? I **think** she's crazy.*
    *This **belongs** to me. It **looks** like a bomb.*
  - to describe timetabled or fixed events:
    *The exams **start** next Monday.*

No, _fish_ swim.
Birds _fly_.

## 2 Simple past

Time: before now
Viewpoint: a completed act

- Use the simple past:
  - to make statements about the past
    *The police **wanted** to know how the fire **started**.*
  - to tell a story
    *When I **was** young, I **had** a pet alligator that **lived** under the stairs and **ate** cornflakes.*
  - with verbs that describe mental states, possession, measurement, appearance:
    *Did you **remember** to lock the door?*
    *I once **owned** a horse that **weighed** a ton.*

### used to

- Use *used to* to emphasise a past habit:
  *I **used to like** rock, but now I prefer jazz.*

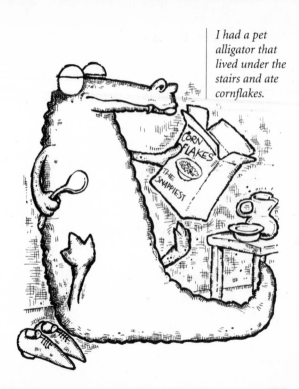

I had a pet alligator that lived under the stairs and ate cornflakes.

# 3 Continuous tenses

Time: shown by part of *be* (*is/was/has been*, etc.)
Viewpoint: an unfinished action, one in progress

- Use a part of *be* with the *-ing* form of the verb:
  *She's **waiting** for her friend to arrive.*
  *I **was leaving** when the phone rang.*

- The present continuous describes:
  - things happening now or in this period of time:
    *I'm **not feeling** well.*
    *James **is studying** to be an accountant.*
  - something planned to happen soon:
    *We're **all going** to a party tomorrow night.*
  - a temporary situation:
    *Why **are you being** so difficult?*

- The past continuous describes background actions in an account of past events:
  *The spectators **were standing** round, chatting and waiting for the race to begin. Suddenly, a man jumped over the fence and ran towards the horses. He **was carrying** a gun …*

*I was sitting in the dentist's waiting room when I heard a loud scream.*

## 4 Perfect tenses

Time: between a point in the past and now, exact time is not given
Viewpoint: result of the action more important than the time when it happened

- Use *has/have* + the past participle:
  *Look, Anna **has left** her books behind!*
  *Have you seen George lately?*

- Use the continuous form if
- the action is still going on:
  *I **have been waiting** here for ages!*
- you can see the results of a recent action:
  *It **has been raining**: the roads are still wet.*

- Use *had* for the past perfect:
  *I noticed that Anna **had left** her books behind.*
  *If I **had left** later, I would have missed my bus.*

# 5 Ways of expressing the future

Time: later than now
Viewpoint: fixed, planned, predicted, etc.

- Use *will* in statements of fact:
  *It **will snow** soon.*
  *If you sit down, you **will be** more comfortable.*

- Use present simple for a regular planned event:
  *The concert **starts** at 8, and **finishes** at 10.*

- Use present continuous for a planned but not regular event:
  *A new supermarket **is opening** next week.*

- Use *going to*
  - to make personal predictions:
    *It's **going to snow**. Just look at the sky!*
  - to emphasise intentions:
    *Charlie says he's **going to drop out of** college.*

# Practice 6

**A** **Choose the correct form to complete the sentences.**

1 What (do you do/are you doing) with a bottle opener? I'm going to open a bottle, silly!

2 What (do you do/are you doing) with a bottle opener? You open bottles, silly!

3 Why (don't you work/aren't you working)? It's my coffee break.

4 Why (don't you work/aren't you working)? I don't need to, I'm rich.

5 This bottle (holds/is holding) 2 litres.

6 We (hold/are holding) a meeting later on.

**B** **Make sentences by matching 1–4 with a–d.**

| | |
|---|---|
| 1 Are you coming to the party | a) tonight |
| 2 Everybody's going to the party | b) every Friday |
| 3 I go cycling | c) on Friday |
| 4 I'm going cycling | d) most Fridays |

## C Match 1–4 with a–d.

1 I wanted to see Ann but
2 You can't see Ann because
3 I managed to see Ann just as
4 I managed to see Ann just before

a) she left.
b) she was leaving.
c) she has already left.
d) she had already left.

## D Match 1–4 with a–d.

1 Ann has been in bed
2 Ann always used to go to bed
3 Ann was just going to bed
4 Ann never goes to bed

a) at 9 o'clock.
b) before setting her alarm clock.
c) since 9 o'clock.
d) when the phone rang.

*Anne always puts the cat out when she goes to bed.*

# Review 6

**Correct the following sentences. There may be more than one mistake in each sentence.**

1 ✗ I'm not sure what is the H standing for in $H_2O$.

_____

2 ✗ We go to Rome last year and see the Vatican.

_____

3 ✗ I was being a good singer when I was younger.

_____

4 ✗ 'I've lost my purse.' 'What is it looking like?'

_____

5 ✗ When was the Golden Gate bridge erecting?

_____

6 ✗ 'Why we won't go shopping tomorrow?' 'OK.'

_____

7 ✗ Do you think it rains this evening?

_____

8 ✗ I'm waiting for you since long time.

_____

# Verbs 3: Other forms

# Key facts about modals

**must/have (got) to**

- Use *must*
  - to express obligation:
    *You **must** say nothing; you **mustn't** tell anyone!*
  - to express a positive logical deduction
    *He **must** be ill: he hasn't eaten anything.*

- Use *have/had (got) to* for other tenses:
  *We **had to** walk to school when I was young.*

- Use *don't have to* (or *don't need to*)
  to express no obligation:
  *You **don't have to** tell me; I already know.*

**should/ought to**

- Use *should/ought to*
  - to say you expect something to happen:
    *If you turn the key, the engine **should** start.*
  - to say it is better to do/not to do something:
    *You **shouldn't** eat so much chocolate!*

**can** (past and conditional: **could**)

- Use *can/could*
  - to express ability/possibility:
    *I **could** read when I was only three years old.*
  - to express a negative logical deduction:
    *You **can't** be serious! You must be joking!*
  - to make a polite request:
    ***Could** you pass the salt, please?*

## may/might

- Use *may/might*
  - to say you are not certain if something will happen or not (*might* is less certain than *may*):
    *I **may** see you tomorrow if I'm not too busy.*
    *I **might** see you tomorrow, but it's very unlikely.*
  - to express a polite request or ask permission:
    ***May** I have another cake, please?*

# Key facts about conditionals

A conditional sentence has at least two clauses, one containing a **condition** and the other containing a **consequence**.

### Tenses in conditional sentences

- Use clauses beginning with *if* to say how the condition leads to the consequence:
  - in the world as it is: *If you kiss me, I'll scream.*
  - in the world as it might be (but isn't): *If I had a million dollars, I would buy a yacht.*
  - in the world as it might have been (but wasn't): *If I had gone to university, I would be rich now.*

 Where *if* means *every time*, use the present simple in both parts of the sentence:
*If you heat water, it boils.*

# Key facts about passives

- Use part of *be* + the past participle:
  *The road **has been blocked** by snow.*
  *The car **was taken** without permission.*

- Use the passive
  – to put the most important element first:
  *Several bystanders **were killed** by gunmen.*
  (rather than '*Gunmen killed several bystanders.*')
  – when the person performing the action is not important, or is not known:
  *If it rains, the picnic **will be cancelled**.*

 Note how the indirect object can become the subject of a passive sentence:
*They never told us the truth – We were never told the truth.*
*Someone sent him a fax – He was sent a fax.*

# Key facts about gerunds and infinitives

- Gerunds can be the subject or the object:
  *Walking is good for you. I enjoy walking.*
  Use the gerund:
  - after prepositions
    *She's very good **at remembering** dates.*
  - after certain verbs, e.g. *dislike, enjoy, keep on*:
    *We just **kept (on) working**.*
  - in the expression *It's no use/good.*
    *It's **no good talking** to him. He's deaf.*

- Use the infinitive without *to*:
  - after modals:
    *I **must go**. I **can't wait** any longer.*
  - after *let* and *make*:
    *Please **let me go**. Don't **make me stay** here.*
  - with 'sense' verbs (*feel, hear, see, watch*):
    *I **felt** someone **touch** my shoulder.*

- Use the infinitive with *to*
  - to express intention:
    *I work long hours **to pay** my children's school fees.*
  - after certain verbs, e.g. *agree, decide, hope, promise, teach, want, wish*:
    *I want to **learn to drive**. Please **teach** me **to drive**.*

- Some verbs may be followed by the gerund or by the infinitive with a change of meaning:
  *We **stopped to ask** the way./Please **stop talking**.*
  *Did you **remember to put** the cat out?/I don't **remember buying** this dress!*

  In other cases there is very little difference of meaning:
  *I **hate writing** letters./I **hate to say** this, but …*
  *It **started to rain**./It **started raining** at dawn.*

# Practice 7

**A** **Use *can't be*, *must be*, *can't have* or *must have* in these sentences.**

1 How old is Linda? She has grey hair, so she ....
over 40.

2 Who took the file? It .... been Joe, he's the only
one with a key to the filing cabinet.

3 She .... over 40! I'm older than her and I'm only
35.

4 Who took the file? It .... been Alicia. She
doesn't have a key.

**B** **Use *mustn't* or *don't have to* in these sentences.**

1 You .... come with us if you don't want to.

2 You can look at my toys, but you .... touch
anything.

3 It's a secret, you .... tell anyone else, OK?

4 You .... shout, I'm not deaf!

**C Use *should/shouldn't be* to say what's wrong.**

1 him            There .... a dot over the i.
2 english     The word english ....
                     written with a capital letter
3 180kph!!!!!!    That car .... travelling at
                     180kph. It's dangerous.
4 No Smoking    Those people .... smoking in
                     here. Can't they read?

**D Choose the correct phrase to complete the sentences.**

1 He's good at ...       a) ... playing the guitar
2 Let them ...           b) ... to play the guitar
3 Just keep on ...       c) ... play the guitar
4 I dislike ...
5 Julia hates ...
6 We enjoy ...
7 You can't make me ...
8 I'd like ...

# Review 7

**Correct the following sentences. There may be more than one mistake in each sentence.**

1 ✗ Did you enjoyed to dance with my girlfriend?

2 ✗ If you will not be busy, I might to can see you later.

3 ✗ If you're very good, I might to let you coming with me.

4 ✗ If there will not be enough enrolments, the course will cancel.

5 ✗ We saw that the door was locked, so we can't get in.

6 ✗ To us was not told the truth.

7 ✗ I saw the car to crash into a wall.

# Adverbials

# 8

# Key facts about adverbials

- Adverbials say something more about the action or state described by a verb:
  *run quickly, be in trouble*

- They modify adjectives:
  *good – very good*; *nice – quite nice*;
  *great – really great*

- They relate to
  **manner**: the question *How?*
  **place**: the question *Where (to)?*
  **time**: the questions *When? How long?*
  **frequency**: the question *How often?*

- Adverbials can be:
  – a word (i.e. an adverb) *You should **always** tell the truth.*
  – a phrase *He spoke **in an American accent**.*
  – a whole clause *I go to bed **when I am tired**.*

## Comparisons

We usually use *more* and *less* to make comparisons of adverbs:
*You should drive **more carefully** at night.*
*Can you talk a little **less loudly**?*

Note: *hard–harder, fast–faster, well–better, badly–worse*
*Tea tastes better if you don't add sugar.*

# 1 Manner

- Add -*ly* to adjectives:
  *sad–sadly*; *happy–happily*; *terrible–terribly*
  *I am happy to tell you/I will **happily** tell you*
  *Good* changes to *well*; *hard* and *fast* do not change:
  *He's a good driver: he drives **well**.*
  *He drives carefully; he never drives **fast**.*

- Avoid putting the adverb between a verb and its object:
  *She **quickly left** the room; not She **left quickly** the room.*

- Note the position of the adverb in verbs using parts of *have* and *be* or modals:
  *He has **definitely** left the building.*
  *They were **carefully** counting the money.*
  *She will **probably** make a mistake.*
  *You might **easily** have missed the bus.*

- An adverbial at the beginning of a sentence is like a comment on the whole sentence:
  ***Gently**, Sarah picked up the injured bird.*
  ***On the whole**, I think women are better drivers.*

*I'm afraid, Mr Jones, that you have definitely failed your driving test …*

## 2 Place

> here, there, upstairs, downstairs, next door, upside down,
> back to front, face to face, side by side, up and down,
> backwards, forwards

- The most common adverbials of place are *here*
  and *there*:

  *Bring it **here**.*
  ***Here** it is!*
  *Put it over **there**.*
  ***There's** a hole in your shirt.*

- Many adverbials of place are phrases:

  *Why did you hang mother's picture **upside
  down**?*
  *You've got your T-shirt on **back to front**.*

- Words ending in *-wards* relate to movement:
  *The rope swung **backwards** and **forwards**.*

## 3 Time

- Time adverbials can relate to
  - a point of time:
  *See you **tomorrow at six in the morning**.*
  - a length of time:
  *Will you stay in London **the whole week**?*

- The order of time adverbials is usually:
  - from the particular to the general
  *I was born **on Friday, the fifth of June, 1985**.*
  - how long, how often
  *The Board meets **for an hour every morning**.*
  - day + time (focus on the time)
  *Let's meet **on Friday at 9**.*
  - time + day (focus on the day)
  *Let's meet **at 9 on Friday**.*

 The normal order of adverbials is manner, place and time: *He went quietly out of the house at midnight.*

# 4 Frequency

> never, rarely, seldom, occasionally, sometimes, often,
> usually, generally, always

- Frequency adverbs range from *never* through
  *sometimes* and *often* to *always*:
  *I've **never** liked tea; I **always** drink coffee.*

- The normal position is before the part of the
  verb that carries the main meaning:
  *You can **usually identify** a bird by its song.*

- Put adverbs of frequency at the beginning or
  end of the sentence if you want to draw
  attention to them:
  ***Usually**, birds don't sing in the wintertime (but
  there are some exceptions!)*
  *She doesn't lose her temper **often** (but when she
  does ... !!!)*

- If you put *seldom* or *rarely* at the beginning of
  the sentence, invert the verb:
  *I have **seldom** heard such nonsense, but
  **Seldom** have I heard such nonsense!*

*She doesn't lose her temper often, but when she does …*

## A note on adverbial clauses

- Adverbial clauses of place are introduced by:
  *as far as, where, wherever, everywhere*

  *This is **as far as** I go.*
  *We will find him **wherever** he may be.*

- Adverbial clauses of time are introduced by:
  *after, as, as long as, as soon as, before,*
  *now that, once, since, until, when,*
  *whenever, while*

  *Stay **as long as** you like. Go **before** it gets dark.*

- Other adverbial clauses are introduced by:
  *although, as far as, as long as (providing),*
  *as if, because, in case, so that*

  *You look **as if** you had seen a ghost!*
  *Take some water **in case** you get thirsty.*

# Practice 8

## A Complete the table.

|   | ADJECTIVE | ADVERB |
|---|-----------|--------|
| 1 | nice | |
| 2 | | usefully |
| 3 | angry | |
| 4 | | terribly |
| 5 | real | |
| 6 | | easily |

## B Match each verb with an adverb.

| 1 breathe | a) brightly |
|-----------|-------------|
| 2 shine | b) clearly |
| 3 sleep | c) deeply |
| 4 speak | d) patiently |
| 5 wait | e) softly |
| 6 whisper | f) soundly |

**C** **Match each verb with an adverb.**

| | | | |
|---|---|---|---|
| 1 | behave | a) | angrily |
| 2 | eat | b) | attentively |
| 3 | listen | c) | badly |
| 4 | shout | d) | gently |
| 5 | remember | e) | greedily |
| 6 | stroke | f) | suddenly |

**D** **Put the adverbials into these sentences.**

1 Haven't you seen an elephant fly? (ever)
2 Make sure you close the door. (quietly)
3 He doesn't make such a fuss. (usually)
4 We stay in bed late on Sundays. (always)
5 Where's Jane? She's in her study. (probably)
6 John has gone out. (just)

**E Choose the correct expression.**

1 Take your umbrella (in case/so that) it rains.

2 Let's go (before/until) he changes his mind!

3 This dog follows me (where/wherever) I go.

4 Are you ill? You look (as if/as) you have flu.

5 Wait here (while/since) I go to the bank.

6 You can stay (as long as/as far as) you like.

**F Match the numbers with the letters to make sentences.**

1 ① he has been ② ③
   a) on business   b) apparently   c) abroad

2 She ① works ② ③
   a) always   b) in the morning   c) much better

3 I ① sleep ② ③
   a) well   b) in a strange bed   c) never

4 You should ① park ② ③
   a) after dark   b) without lights   c) never

# Review 8

**Correct the following sentences. There may be more than one mistake in each sentence.**

1 ✗ Barbara speaks fluently French.

_____

2 ✗ Try to think in future more careful before you speak.

_____

3 ✗ John works very hardly; he takes never a holiday.

_____

4 ✗ Have you still finished your homework?

_____

5 ✗ I would go never by car to work.

_____

6 ✗ Be carefully when you ever cross the road.

_____

# Frequently asked questions

9

# Q1 What's the difference between *make* and *do*?

## Make

- Literally, *make* describes creating or producing something from raw materials: *I made a model house out of toothpicks.*
- We use *make* metaphorically in expressions like: *make a mistake, make friends, make a noise.*

**Common expressions with *make***
*make* ... a profit/loss, a phone call, a speech, a decision, an impression, a fuss, an appointment, a suggestion, an excuse, a complaint, an offer, a plan, arrangements, changes, progress

## Do

- Literally, *do* describes performing an action on something which already exists: *do a crossword, do your hair* (i.e. brush it).

**Common expressions with *do***
*do* ... your hair, your best, your duty, well, someone a favour, business, a good job, harm, the/some shopping; it will do you good

## Q2 How do I use *get/have something done*?

- Use this pattern when you ask or pay someone else to do a job for you:
  *I need to get/have the car serviced.*
  *Where do you get/have your hair done?*

- Use the pattern with *get* for something you will do yourself, but which will take a lot of effort:
  *I really must get this essay finished!*

- If you name the person, the pattern is:
  *I must get Mervyn to service my car*
  or (less usual)
  *I must have Mervyn service my car.*

## Q3 What's the difference between *say* and *tell*?

- *To tell* is to inform or to order (include the person who is being told):
  *Tell me your name. Tell the children to be quiet.*

   Note the expressions: *tell a story, tell the time.*

- *To say* is to utter words:
  *The children said 'Thank you, grandma!'*
  *Grandma said 'I am very proud of you!'*

- We can also report what has been said:
  *The children said thank you to their grandma, and grandma said that she was very proud of them.*

   Note the different pattern:
  *I told **her** (that) I was upset.*
  *I said **to her** (that) I was upset.*

# Q4 What's the difference between *still* and *yet*?

They both mean 'up to the present time'.

- *Still* describes something that has been happening, and may be continuing:
  *I still work for IBM.*
  *Do you still love me?*

- *Yet* describes something that hasn't started (or may not have started) to happen, so it is used only in negative statements and questions:
  *The morning post hasn't arrived yet.*
  *Has the dog been fed yet?*

- Use *still* (with stress) in negative statements to express surprise:
  *Unbelievable! The post **still** hasn't arrived!*

## Q5 What's the difference between *which?* and *what?*

- Use *which?* to ask *which one(s)?* (from a known set of objects).
  *We've got three kinds of apples. Which (ones) do you want?*
  *Which John Grisham novels have you read?*

- Use *what?* to ask a general question:
  *What (kind of) novels do you enjoy reading?*

## Q6 What is the difference between *like doing* and *like to do*?

- *Like doing* focuses on a regular habit:
  *I like reading.*

- *Like to do* focuses on each example of the activity:
  *I like to read for an hour before I go to sleep.*

 Use only *to do* after *would like*: What would you like to eat? I'd like to order a pizza.

## Q7 What's the difference between *must* and *have (got) to*?

- *Must* expresses an obligation from within you:
  *I must remember to buy a birthday card for my sister.*

- *Have to* expresses an obligation from outside:
  *The teacher says we have to (we've got to) work harder.*

Note: *mustn't* expresses an obligation **not** to do.
*Don't have to* means there is no obligation to do.
*You must be nice to her, but you don't have to like her!*

## Q8 What's the difference between *ought to* and *should*?

- *Ought* expresses what you feel you owe to other people (*ought* is an old past form of *owe*).

- *Should* expresses what you feel you owe to yourself.

## Q9 When do I use *shall*?

- *Shall* is usually used only with *I* or *we*. The most common use is in questions:

  *Shall I open the window?*
  *Shall we go now?*

## Q10 What's the difference between *very* and *too*?

- *Very* expresses a higher degree of a quality:
  *This tea is hot; in fact, it's very hot.*

- *Too* expresses an unacceptable degree:
  *If it's very hot, I **can** still drink it, but if it's too hot, I **can't** drink it.*

# Common errors

**Now that you have almost completed the book, see how many of these common errors you can correct. There may be more than one mistake in each sentence.**

1 ✗ John is teacher.
2 ✗ I fell and broke the leg, so I must to go to hospital.
3 ✗ I go always to the work on bus.
4 ✗ Nobody helped me: I did it all by my own.
5 ✗ I never said nothing to nobody.
6 ✗ What time the bus leaves for Oxford?
7 ✗ Why you don't get your hair cutting?
8 ✗ She left house without saying me goodbye.
9 ✗ I am waiting since ages! Where you been?

10  ✗ Here's a picture from a dog and it's owner.

11  ✗ Are you believing for ghosts?

12  ✗ Alicia: I don't like people which smokes.

13  ✗ Philip: Neither I do.

14  ✗ You shouldn't of eaten so much potatoes.

15  ✗ She is the beautifullest girl I am knowing.

16  ✗ If I were you, I would listen your fathers advices.

17  ✗ I made my homeworks in less than an hour!

18  ✗ Jack should be here an hour ago, and he hasn't still arrived!

19  ✗ I am very interesting in Indian music.

20  ✗ Have another drink: it won't make you no harm.

# Grammar files

# Grammar file 1: Prepositional phrases

## A  Verbs followed by particular prepositions

| | | |
|---|---|---|
| account for | come from | look like |
| accuse of | congratulate on | long for |
| agree with | depend on | object to |
| apologise for | escape from | pay for |
| approve of | get rid of | prevent from |
| arrive at | hope for | rely on |
| ask for | laugh at | reply to |
| be/get used to | listen to | see to |
| believe in | look after | stare at |
| belong to | look at | suffer from |
| blame for | look for | take after |
| borrow from | look forward to | (wouldn't) dream of |

Use the *-ing* form of the verb after a preposition:
*I don't believe in getting up early.*
*I wouldn't dream of doing that!*

# B Adjectives followed by particular prepositions

absent from

accustomed/used to

afraid of

angry about

ashamed of

aware of

bad at

close to

different from/to

fond of

full of

glad about

good at

grateful for

interested in

jealous of

keen on

late for

mad/crazy about

pleased with

proud of

ready for

sad about

serious about

similar to

sorry about

sorry for

surprised at

tired of

worried about

# Grammar file 2: Verb patterns

## Simple tenses

| I/we/you/they | (don't) | sing |
| | (didn't) | |
| | | sang |
| he/she/it | | sings |
| | | sang |
| | doesn't | sing |
| | didn't | |

## Perfect tenses

| I/we/you/they | have | talked |
| | had | |
| he/she/it | has | |
| | had | |

## Continuous tenses

| | | |
|---|---|---|
| I | am | singing |
| | was | |
| | have been | |
| he/she/it | is | |
| | was | |
| | has been | |
| we/you/they | are | |
| | were | |
| | have been | |
| I/he/she/it/ we/you/they | had been | |
| | will be | |
| | must (etc.) be | |

## Passives

| | am | |
| I | was | |
| | have been | |
| | is | |
| he/she/it | was | called |
| | has been | |
| | are | |
| we/you/they | were | |
| | have been | |
| I/he/she/it/ we/you/they | had been | |

 Continuous passives are possible but not common:
*Something is being done.*
*We were being criticised.*

# Grammar file 3: Common irregular verbs

## Pattern ABC

### 1 Changing to -*o*- in simple past tense

| | | |
|---|---|---|
| break | broke | broken |
| choose | chose | chosen |
| drive | drove | driven |
| forget | forgot | forgotten |
| freeze | froze | frozen |
| speak | spoke | spoken |
| steal | stole | stolen |
| tear | tore | torn |
| wear | wore | worn |

### 2 Changing to -*oo*- in simple past tense

| | | |
|---|---|---|
| shake | shook | shaken |
| take | took | taken |

## 3 Changing to -e- in simple past tense

| | | |
|---|---|---|
| blow | blew | blown |
| draw | drew | drawn |
| fall | fell | fallen |
| fly | flew | flown |
| go | went | gone |
| grow | grew | grown |
| know | knew | known |
| throw | threw | thrown |

## 4 Changing to -i- in simple past tense

| | | |
|---|---|---|
| bite | bit | bitten |
| do | did | done |
| hide | hid | hidden |

## 5 Changing to -a- in simple past tense

| be | was | been |
| eat | ate | eaten |
| forgive | forgave | forgiven |
| give | gave | given |
| lie | lay | lain |
| see | saw | seen |
| begin | began | begun |
| drink | drank | drunk |
| sing | sang | sung |
| swim | swam | swum |

This verb is also ABC but does not fit any of the above categories:

*show      showed      shown*

## Pattern ABB

### 1 Ending in -*d*

| have | had | had |
| hear | heard | heard |
| hold | held | held |
| lay | laid | laid |
| make | made | made |
| pay | paid | paid |
| say | said | said |
| sell | sold | sold |
| stand | stood | stood |
| tell | told | told |
| feed | fed | fed |
| lead | led | led |
| read | read | read |
| find | found | found |

## 2 Ending in -t

| | | |
|---|---|---|
| bend | bent | bent |
| build | built | built |
| feel | felt | felt |
| get | got | got |
| keep | kept | kept |
| leave | left | left |
| lend | lent | lent |
| lose | lost | lost |
| mean | meant | meant |
| meet | met | met |
| send | sent | sent |
| shoot | shot | shot |
| sit | sat | sat |
| sleep | slept | slept |
| spend | spent | spent |

## 3 Ending in *-ought/-aught*

| | | |
|---|---|---|
| bring | brought | brought |
| buy | bought | bought |
| catch | caught | caught |
| fight | fought | fought |
| teach | taught | taught |
| think | thought | thought |

## 4 Vowel change *-i/-a* to *-u/-o*

| | | |
|---|---|---|
| dig | dug | dug |
| hang | hung | hung |
| stick | stuck | stuck |
| strike | struck | struck |
| shine | shone | shone |
| win | won | won |

# Pattern AAA

| | | |
|---|---|---|
| bet | bet | bet |
| cost | cost | cost |
| cut | cut | cut |
| hit | hit | hit |
| hurt | hurt | hurt |
| let | let | let |
| put | put | put |
| set | set | set |
| split | split | split |
| spread | spread | spread |
| shut | shut | shut |

## Other patterns

| | | |
|---|---|---|
| become | became | become |
| come | came | come |
| run | ran | run |
| beat | beat | beaten |

# Answers

## 1 Nouns and pronouns

### Practice: 1A

**A** 1 woman  2 lives  3 foot  4 children  5 days  6 lady
7 matches  8 books  9 tax  10 trees

**B** 1 are  2 costs  3 is  4 looks  5 have

**C** 1 armchair  2 bottle opener  3 greenhouse
4 matchstick  5 police car  6 post office  7 screwdriver
8 telephone directory  9 wristwatch

### Practice: 1B

**A**

| I | me | my | mine | myself |
|---|-----|------|-------|---------------------|
| you | you | your | yours | yourself/yourselves |
| he | him | his | his | himself |
| she | her | her | hers | herself |
| it | it | its | – | itself |
| we | us | our | ours | ourselves |
| they | them | their | theirs | themselves |

**B** 1 my  2 her  3 ourselves  4 their  5 me  6 yours

**Review 1**

1 Did she go to the party on her own/by herself? 2 It's/It is time to give the cat its dinner. 3 Look after yourselves, children! 4 Explain to me the difference between *if* and *when*. 5 Is this your hairbrush? 6 There's not/There isn't much bread left. 7 Did Kate tell you/Did Kate say where she was going? 8 Your house is bigger than ours.

## 2 Determiners
**Practice 2**

**A** 1 French people shake hands more often than the English do/than English people do. 2 The Moon goes round the Earth. 3 Let me give you a piece of advice: don't accept sweets from strange men! 4 When I was a boy, we always had eggs for breakfast. 5 What time do you leave home in the morning? 6 *If* is a poem by an English writer.

**B** 1 There's no point in telling me; I can't do anything about it. 2 Somebody's been smoking! I can smell it! 3 I have coffee but no milk, so you'll have to drink it black. 4 Shall I make some more popcorn for you? 5 I know hardly anybody at this party.

**Review 2**

**A** 1 Is this money yours? 2 There aren't any cakes/There are no cakes left. The cat has eaten them all/all of them.

3 We do some shopping every weekend.  4 I have three
sons and they are all crazy.  5 Have you lived here all your
life? 6 Why do the French/Why do French people always
shake hands when they meet?

**B** 1 I need a little more time.  2 You should eat less bread.
3 There isn't much furniture in here.  4 I haven't many
exercises to do.

## 3 Adjectivals
### Practice 3

**A** 1 all my old school photos 2 several old French dining
tables 3 Mike's first African wildlife safari 4 a lot of pretty
young Brazilian girls 5 a pair of white cotton tennis shorts

**B** (Sample answers) 1 Japanese is more difficult than
English. 2 Walking is healthier than jogging. 3 Thirst is
worse than hunger. 4 Health is more important than
money. 5 Half a loaf is better than no loaf at all.

**C** 1 fall asleep 2 go mad 3 grow old 4 make sure
5 stand still 6 turn green

**D** 1 I am the girl (that) you wrote to. 2 I am the only one
who/that can speak Chinese. 3 She's the one who/that
works in a bank. 4 He's the man (that) I told you about.
5 This is the cat that/which ate my breakfast.

**Review 3**

1 Never wake up a sleeping tiger (a tiger that is asleep).
2 It's the biggest stadium in the world! 3 Are you the man whose cat ate my breakfast? 4 I am interested in football. I go to all the matches. 5 Today is the twenty-second of June. 6 Angela is the most intelligent person I know.

## 4 Prepositions

### Practice 4A

**A** 1 across 2 past 3 round 4 up 5 over 6 through 7 across 8 along 9 over 10 into

**B** 1 I last ate at seven o'clock. I haven't eaten since seven o'clock. I haven't eaten for five hours. 2 I was born in 1980. I was born on Friday 7 July at 3 o'clock in the morning!

### Practice 4B

1 a present for/on your birthday 2 a painting by Rembrandt 3 a table made of/from wood 4 an old man with a grey beard 5 a car that goes like the wind 6 a book about dinosaurs 7 a building taller than the Eiffel Tower 8 a peace march against the war 9 I am very proud of my daughter. 10 He is very good at football. 11 Did you pay for the meal? 12 Does this pen belong to you? 13 Bill looks exactly like his father! 14 I'm not used to eating spicy food. 15 Do you believe in ghosts?

**Review 4**

**A** 1 Please be home by 10 pm at the latest!  2 I have been waiting for two hours.  3 John got tired of waiting, so he went home.  4 Our friends were late, so we went without them.  5 What did you do at the weekend?  6 12.50 is the same as ten to one.  7 We arrived at the hotel after midnight.

**B** 1c  2d  3f  4e  5a  6b

## 5 Verbs 1: Form

**Practice 5**

**A**

| | | |
|---|---|---|
| 1 | find | found | found |
| 2 | catch | caught | caught |
| 3 | fall | fell | fallen |
| 4 | put | put | put |
| 5 | see | saw | seen |
| 6 | write | wrote | written |
| 7 | tell | told | told |
| 8 | take | took | taken |
| 9 | meet | met | met |
| 10 | cost | cost | cost |

**B** 1 Where did you go last night?  2 Where do you live?  3 What did you have for dinner?  4 How many languages can you speak?  5 How do you go to work?  6 Which program do you use?  7 What have you done today?

C 1 It has moved – It has been moved – It has been moving – It will move  2 Does she work? – Did she work? – Has she worked? – Is she working?

## Review 5

1 What does John do? He teaches physics.  2 I'm tired: I've been working hard.  3 Must we stay in?  4 Why doesn't this watch work?  5 You're a student, aren't you?  6 Can you tell me the time, please?  7 This box measures 200cm by 300cm.  8 Do you live here? Yes, I do.

## 6 Verbs 2: Tenses

### Practice 6

A 1 are you doing  2 do you do  3 aren't you working  4 don't you work  5 holds  6 are holding

B 1 + a/c  2 + a/c  3 + b/d  4 + a/c

C 1d 2c 3b 4a

D  1c 2a 3d 4b (a is also correct)

## Review 6

1 I'm not sure what the H stands for in $H_2O$.  2 We went to Rome last year and saw the Vatican.  3 I was a good singer when I was younger.  4 'I've lost my purse.' 'What does it look like?'  5 When was the Golden Gate Bridge

erected? 6 'Why don't we go shopping tomorrow?' 'OK.'
7 Do you think it will rain/it's going to rain this evening?
8 I've been waiting for you (for) a long time.

## 7 Verbs 3: Other forms

### Practice 7

**A** 1 must be  2 must have  3 can't be  4 can't have
**B** 1 don't have to  2 mustn't  3 mustn't  4 don't have to
**C** 1 should be  2 should be  3 shouldn't be  4 shouldn't be
**D** 1a  2c  3a  4a  5a or b  6a  7c  8b

### Review 7

1 Did you enjoy dancing with my girlfriend?
2 If you are/you're not busy, I might be able to see you
later.  3 If you're very good, I might let you come with
me.  4 If there aren't enough enrolments, the course will
be cancelled.  5 We saw that the door was locked, so we
couldn't get in.  6 We were not told the truth.  7 I saw the
car crash into a wall.

## 8 Adverbials

### Practice 8

**A** 1 nicely  2 useful  3 angrily  4 terrible  5 really  6 easy
**B** 1c  2a  3f  4b (e also fits)  5d  6e
**C** 1c  2e  3b  4a  5f  6d

**D** 1 Haven't you ever seen an elephant fly?  2 Make sure you close the door quietly.  3 He doesn't usually/He usually doesn't make such a fuss.  4 We always stay in bed late on Sundays.  5 Where's Jane? She's probably in her study.  6 John has just gone out.

**E** 1 in case  2 before  3 wherever  4 as if  5 while 6 as long as

**F** 1 Apparently he has been abroad on business.  2 She always works much better in the morning.  3 I never sleep well in a strange bed.  4 You should never park without lights after dark.

## Review 8

1 Barbara speaks French fluently. 2 Try to think more carefully in future before you speak/In future, try to think more carefully ∴ 3 John works very hard; he never takes a holiday. 4 Have you finished your homework yet? 5 I would never go to work by car. 6 Be careful whenever you cross the road.

## 9 Frequently asked questions

### Common errors

1 John is a teacher. 2 I fell and broke my leg, so I must go to hospital. 3 I always go to work by bus/on the bus. 4 Nobody helped me: I did it all by myself/on my own.

5 I never said anything to anybody.  6 What time does the bus leave for Oxford?  7 Why don't you get your hair cut?  8 She left the house without saying goodbye to me.
9 I have been waiting for ages! Where have you been?
10 Here's a picture of a dog and its owner.  11 Do you believe in ghosts?  12 Alicia: I don't like people who/that smoke.  13 Philip: Neither do I.  14 You shouldn't have eaten so many potatoes.  15 She is the most beautiful girl I know.  16 If I were you, I would listen to your father's advice.  17 I did my homework in less than an hour!
18 Jack should have been here an hour ago, and he still hasn't arrived!  19 I am very interested in Indian music.
20 Have another drink: it won't do you any harm.